WE DON'T KNOW WHO NEEDS TO HEAR THIS BUT ...

40 Devotionals to Uplift, Inspire, and Encourage

DANIELLE ROBINSON SMITH
AND GLENN E. COLEMAN

Copyright © 2024 By Danielle Robinson Smith

All rights reserved. This book or any portion thereof may not be reproduced or used in any manner whatsoever without written permission from the authors, Danielle Robinson Smith or Glenn E. Coleman, except for the use of brief quotations in a book review.

Contact: info@graceandgritlg.com

The information contained within this book is strictly for educational purposes. If you wish to apply the ideas herein, you take full responsibility for your actions. The guidance provided within this book was developed based on the personal experiences and opinions of the authors. The authors do not assume and hereby disclaim any liability to any party for any loss, damage, or disruption caused by errors or omissions, whether such errors or omissions result from accident, negligence, or any other cause.

ISBN: 979-8-9918507-0-4
Printed in the United States of America

Book Cover Design and Interior Formatting by 100Covers.

Table of Contents

Build up your Courage and Strength...1
You have Courage and Strength for any Situation...........................3
Keep Walking in Faith 7
Let It Go..11
Grace is Yours 17
Change is Inevitable, but Growth is Optional.................................21
Blessed and Highly Favored 25
Be Decisive vs Acting in Haste (Slow Down but Don't Stop) 29
Response vs. Reaction 33
Finding Peace Amidst Anxiety..37
Vision Without Execution is a Mirage..39
Model the Way..43
Weapons May Form, but They Won't Succeed 47
Crushing Self-Doubt...51
Embracing Your Worth...53
Trusting God's Timing...55
Overcoming Anxiety 57
Building Strong Relationships 59
Finding Joy in the Journey..61
Forgiveness Sets You Free..63
Trusting God's Plan..65
Embracing Your Identity in Christ..67

Living a Life of Generosity 69

Strength in Weakness 71

Finding Hope in Brokenness 73

Embracing Healing Through Vulnerability 75

Strengthened by Grace 77

Beauty from Ashes: Transforming Brokenness into Beauty 79

Uplifted by God's Promises 81

Strength Through Community 83

Renewed by God's Word 85

Restoration Through Rest 87

Standing on Business, God's Business 89

Be Prepared for Your Purpose 91

Strength in Waiting 93

Going Through the Fire 95

The Eternity in Each Moment 97

Netflix and Chill: Time to Rest 99

Seasons of Waiting 101

Using Time Wisely 103

Discernment 105

About the Authors 111

To those navigating the challenges of everyday life, facing uncertainty, fatigue, and the weight of unspoken burdens. May you find inspiration in the smallest moments and encouragement in the kindness of others. This book is for you, a reminder that your journey matters, that hope can bloom even in the toughest times, and that you are never alone. Keep moving forward; each step is a testament to your strength and resilience.

Introduction

Welcome! I'm so glad you're here, and I truly believe this devotional journey will be life-changing for you. Over the next 40 weeks, you'll dive into a weekly devotional designed to meet you where you are and help you grow in your faith. Each week, you'll find five key elements: Scripture Reading, Reflection, Contemplation, Prayer, and an Action Step. All are thoughtfully woven together to guide you through different seasons of life.

We've broken these devotionals into key themes: Building Courage and Strength, Growth, Trusting God's Timing, Hope, and Forgiveness. Each theme has been chosen with intention, recognizing that we all walk through different challenges and need to lean on God's word in unique ways.

Maybe you're facing a season that requires more courage than you feel you have, or you're struggling to trust God's timing. Whatever it is, these devotionals will help you lean in, press forward, and ultimately grow stronger in your walk with God.

I want to encourage you to do one thing as you go through this: don't rush. Take it week by week. The action steps are designed to give you space to put what you've learned into practice, so use the lines provided to write down your thoughts, goals, or what God's showing you. Reflect on where He's leading you, and allow these exercises to deepen your faith and trust in Him.

Ready? Let's get started. I'm excited to see how God will work in your heart and life over these 40 weeks!

Build up your Courage and Strength

Scripture Reading

- Joshua 1:9 (NIV): "Have I not commanded you? Be strong and courageous. Do not be afraid; do not be discouraged, for the Lord your God will be with you wherever you go."

- Isaiah 40:29 (NIV): "He gives strength to the weary and increases the power of the weak."

Reflection

We Don't Know Who Needs to Hear this, but you are stronger than you know!

Courage and strength are essential virtues that empower us to face life's challenges and fulfill our God-given potential. In Joshua 1:9, God commands Joshua to be strong and courageous as he leads the Israelites into the Promised Land. This command is not merely a call to muster up personal bravery but a reminder that God's presence accompanies us wherever we go. Our courage is rooted in the assurance that God is with us, guiding and supporting us through every trial and uncertainty.

Isaiah 40:29 offers comfort and encouragement by affirming that God provides strength to the weary and empowers the weak. This verse reminds us that our strength is not solely dependent on our efforts but is a gift from God. When we are overwhelmed or exhausted, we can turn to Him for the renewed energy and resilience we need to persevere.

Prayer

Heavenly Father, we come to You today asking for Your courage and strength to face the challenges in our lives. Help us to build our courage and strength on the foundation of Your unwavering presence and power. Grant us the courage to step out in faith, the strength to endure, and the wisdom to recognize Your hand at work in every situation. May our lives be a testament to Your power and grace, shining as a reflection of Your love and guidance.

In Jesus' name, we pray.

Amen.

Contemplation

Reflect on a recent challenge or fear that you have faced. How did you respond to it? Consider how you might invite God into that situation to give you the courage and strength needed. Contemplate how relying on God's power could change your approach to future challenges.

Action Step

Identify a specific area of your life where you need courage and strength. Write down a Scripture that speaks to that need, such as Joshua 1:9 or Isaiah 40:29. Commit to memorizing and meditating on this verse. Take a practical step towards addressing your challenge, such as seeking support, setting a goal, or taking a leap of faith. Regularly pray for God's strength and courage as you move forward, trusting in His provision and guidance.

You have Courage and Strength for any Situation

Scripture Reading

- Deuteronomy 31:6 (KJV): "Be Strong and of a good courage, fear not, nor be afraid of them: for the Lord thy God, he it is that doth go with thee; he will not fail thee, nor forsake thee."

Reflection

We Don't Know Who Needs to Hear this, but your heart is bold and your spirit is strong!

Courage and strength are interrelated and can be developed and reinforced through practice and experience. By embracing these qualities, you can navigate various situations with greater confidence and resilience. Whether personal challenges, professional obstacles, or broader life events, you can draw upon courage and strength in different scenarios:

1. Facing Personal Challenges

Whether dealing with a personal loss, facing a health issue, or making a significant life change, courage means acknowledging your fears but choosing to move forward despite them.

Strength helps you to endure difficulties and recover from setbacks. Building mental and emotional resilience through practices like mindfulness, self-care, and seeking support can enhance your strength.

2. Navigating Professional Obstacles

In a professional setting, courage might mean voicing your ideas, taking calculated risks, or standing up for what you believe is right. Professional strength is demonstrated through your ability to handle stress, adapt to changes, and stay focused on your goals. It is about maintaining your commitment and drive even when faced with challenging projects or difficult colleagues.

Relationship strength involves maintaining empathy, patience, and understanding. It is about being resilient despite disagreements and working through challenges together. Strength in relationships also means setting healthy boundaries and caring for your emotional needs.

Prayer

Heavenly Father, we thank You for the promise of Your unyielding presence and strength as depicted in Deuteronomy 31:6. As we face life's challenges and uncertainties, we ask for the courage to be strong and fearless, knowing that You are with us. Help us to trust in Your unfailing promises, confident that You will never leave nor forsake us. Guide our hearts to lean on this assurance so we may walk boldly in faith, unshaken by adversity. Lord, grant us peace in surrendering our fears to You and empower us to be beacons of Your steadfast love and strength in a world in need.

In Jesus' name, we pray.

Amen.

Contemplation

In contemplating Deuteronomy 31:6, we are drawn to the profound reassurance of God's constant presence and unwavering support. This verse calls us to a steadfast courage that transcends earthly fears, inviting us to a deeper trust in the divine companionship that goes with us wherever we venture. As we quietly sit with these words, we reflect on the times when we have felt alone or overwhelmed and how easy it is to forget that we are enveloped by an inexhaustible love that will never abandon us. This contemplation encourages us to internalize the truth that no matter how formidable our circumstances may appear, the Lord walks with us, offering hope and a profound strength that can see us through any storm. In this sacred stillness, let us open our hearts to embrace the peace and fortitude that comes from knowing we are never truly alone.

Action Step

Life will forever change and continue to throw curveballs; whether planned or unexpected, it simply requires courage to embrace new realities and let go of the old. Adapting to change requires flexibility and persistence. This week, work on managing your emotions, staying positive, and finding new ways to move forward even when things do not go as planned. You have the courage and strength to successfully do it all.

Keep Walking in Faith

Scripture Reading

- ☐ 2 Corinthians 5:7 (NIV): "For we live by faith, not by sight."

- ☐ Hebrews 11:1 (NIV): "Now faith is confidence in what we hope for and assurance about what we do not see."

- ☐ Matthew 17:20 (KJV): "And Jesus said unto them, Because of your unbelief: for verily I say unto you, If ye have faith as a grain of mustard seed, ye shall say unto this mountain, Remove hence to yonder place; and it shall remove; and nothing shall be impossible unto you."

Reflection

We Don't Know Who Needs to Hear this, but your faith is not in vain!

Walking in faith is a fundamental aspect of the Christian journey. It involves navigating life's uncertainties with a trust in God's promises and guidance, even when we cannot see the outcome. Faith is not just belief in God's existence but a profound trust in His character and His plans for our lives.

2 Corinthians 5:7 reminds us that our walk with God is rooted in faith rather than what we can physically see or understand. To walk in faith means to rely on God's wisdom and provision, even when our circumstances seem unclear or challenging. It's an act of trusting in God's promises and His goodness despite our limited perspective.

Hebrews 11:1 defines faith as confidence and assurance in what we hope for but cannot see. This verse underscores that faith involves a deep trust in the unseen, believing God works behind the scenes even when our immediate situation does not reflect it. It's about holding onto hope and assurance that God's plans are for our good, regardless of current evidence.

Prayer

Heavenly Father,

We come before You with hearts seeking to walk more fully in faith. Thank You for the promise that even when we cannot see or understand, You are always at work in our lives. Help us trust in Your plans and live confidently in the hope that You provide. Lord, in times of uncertainty and when we face challenges that test our faith, remind us of Your faithfulness. Teach us to walk not by sight but by the assurance of Your promises. Strengthen our trust in You and help us to remain steadfast, knowing that You are guiding our steps and that Your plans for us are good.

Grant us the courage to step out in faith, even when the path is unclear, and to trust in Your provision and timing. May our lives reflect the confidence and assurance that come with knowing You are in control and that Your love and guidance are always with us.

In Jesus' name, we pray.

Amen.

Contemplation

Consider an area of your life where you struggle to walk in faith. Reflect on how you rely on *your* understanding or sight rather than trusting in God's promises. How can you shift your perspective to walk more confidently in faith, even when the outcome is uncertain?

Action Step

Identify one specific situation where you need to exercise faith. Write down the promises of God that apply to this situation and commit them to memory. Take a deliberate step of faith, such as praying, seeking counsel, or taking a practical action that aligns with your trust in God. Regularly revisit this situation with prayer and reflection, reminding yourself to rely on God's guidance and promises.

LET IT GO

Scripture Reading

- Isaiah 43:18-19 (NIV): "Forget the former things; do not dwell on the past. See, I am doing a new thing! Now it springs up; do you not perceive it? I am making a way in the wilderness and streams in the wasteland."

Reflection

We Don't Know Who Needs to Hear this, but it's time to let it go!

In our fast-paced lives, it's easy to become attached to our routines, possessions, and even past grievances. However, God invites us to consider letting go as essential to growth. Just as nature cycles through seasons, we, too, must release what no longer serves us to make room for new blessings. The concept that "letting go creates space for new" reflects that releasing old or unhelpful elements in your life can open up opportunities for growth and positive change. This principle can be applied to various aspects of life, including personal development, relationships, and professional endeavors. Here's how letting go can create space for new possibilities:

1. Personal Growth

Old Beliefs and Habits: Letting go of outdated or limiting beliefs can free up mental and emotional energy. This openness allows you to adopt new perspectives and develop healthier habits or thought patterns.

Emotional Baggage: Releasing past grievances or unresolved emotions can lead to greater emotional clarity and resilience. This newfound emotional space can enable you to pursue new experiences and relationships with a fresh mindset.

2. Relationships

Toxic Relationships: Letting go of relationships that are harmful or no longer serving you can create room for healthier, more fulfilling connections. By removing these negative influences, you open yourself to relationships that support and uplift you.

Old Patterns: Letting go of unproductive or negative patterns in your interactions with others can lead to more meaningful and positive relationships. This shift can encourage new ways of relating that foster better communication and understanding.

3. Professional Life

Career Transitions: Letting go of a job or career path that no longer aligns with your goals or passions can lead to new opportunities that better fit your skills and aspirations. It can also provide the freedom to explore new fields or roles.

Old Projects or Goals: Releasing outdated projects or goals that no longer serve your current objectives can help you focus on new initiatives that are more relevant and exciting.

4. Physical Space

Decluttering: Letting go of physical clutter can make your living or working space more organized and pleasant. This physical space can enhance your productivity and creativity, allowing you to focus on new projects or activities.

5. Mental Space

Reducing Stress: Letting go of unnecessary stressors or mental preoccupations can improve mental clarity and well-being. This mental space can help you think more creatively and make more intentional decisions.

Practical Steps for Letting Go

Reflect and Assess: Identify what aspects of your life may be holding you back or causing discomfort. Reflect on the impact these elements have on your well-being.

Set Intentions: Clearly define what you want to make space for. This can help you focus your efforts on inviting new opportunities or changes.

Gradual Process: Letting go doesn't always happen overnight. It can be a gradual process involving ongoing adjustments and acceptance.

Seek Support: Sometimes, letting go can be challenging. Seeking support from friends, family, or professionals can provide guidance and encouragement.

Embracing New Possibilities

Once you've made space by letting go, it's important to actively embrace new opportunities. This can involve setting new goals, exploring new interests, and being open to change. Letting go and creating space is not just about removing what no longer serves you but also about actively welcoming and nurturing what can contribute to your growth and fulfillment.

Prayer

Dear Heavenly Father, help me recognize the things I need to release in my life. Please give me the courage to let go of my past, old fears, and any burdens that weigh me down. Open my eyes to the new opportunities and blessings You have in store for me. May I trust in Your plan and embrace the fresh starts that come with each new day.

In Jesus' name, we pray.

Amen.

Contemplation

Take a moment to reflect on what you might be holding onto that prevents you from moving forward. Is there a habit, a fear, or a past disappointment you need to release? Write it down and offer it to God in prayer, asking for His guidance as you create space for new beginnings.

Action Step

This week, take one tangible step toward letting go. Whether it's decluttering a physical space, forgiving someone, or stepping out of your comfort zone, choose to create space for something new. Trust that God is ready to fill that space with His goodness.

GRACE IS YOURS

Scripture Reading

- Ephesians 2:8-9 (NIV): "For it is by grace you have been saved, through faith—and this is not from yourselves, it is the gift of God—not by works, so that no one can boast."

- 2 Corinthians 12:9 (NIV): "But he said to me, 'My grace is sufficient for you, for my power is made perfect in weakness.' Therefore I will boast all the more gladly about my weaknesses, so that Christ's power may rest on me."

- John 1:16 (NIV): "Out of his fullness we have all received grace in place of grace already given."

- 1 Corinthians 15:10 (KJV): "But by the grace of God I am what I am: and his grace which was *bestowed* upon me was not in vain; but I laboured more abundantly than they all: yet not I, but the grace of God which was with me."

Reflection

We Don't Know Who Needs to Hear this, but give yourself some grace!

Grace can be described as the unearned favor of God and is one of the most needed gifts, yet it is so underrated. It is a gift that brings forgiveness, redemption, and spiritual renewal. God gives us grace for our transgressions, yet we often struggle to give grace to others and ourselves. One of the most destructive behaviors often exhibited by high-performing, results-driven individuals is dwelling on what went wrong or what could have been done better. Sound familiar? While reflection is necessary, cathartic, and useful, dwelling on the should've, could've, and would've is not.

In Ephesians 2:8-9, Paul emphasizes that salvation results from God's grace received through faith. This passage reminds us that we are saved not because of our deeds but because of God's generous grace. It is a humbling truth that places our trust in God's provision rather than our own abilities, highlighting the importance of relying on His grace rather than our works.

The power of grace in our weaknesses is revealed in 2 Corinthians 12:9. Paul shares how God's grace is sufficient to cover our deficiencies and struggles. In our weakness, God's grace shines the brightest, demonstrating that His strength is made perfect when we are vulnerable and dependent on Him. This grace empowers us to face challenges, knowing God's strength and support are ever-present.

Prayer

Dear Heavenly Father,

Help us to fully embrace and live in the light of Your grace. Teach us to extend grace to others as freely as You have given it to us. May we be instruments of Your grace, offering kindness, forgiveness, and understanding in our relationships and interactions.

In our moments of weakness and struggle, remind us that Your grace is sufficient. Let us find strength in Your presence, knowing that Your power is made perfect in our vulnerabilities. We trust in Your grace to sustain us and to transform our lives in ways that reflect Your love and goodness.

In Jesus' name, we pray.

Amen.

Contemplation

Over this next week, extend yourself some grace for anything that does not go as planned. While you are great and amazing, *you* are human! Thank God for his never-ending grace, hold your head up high, and keep pushing forward. Reflect on a recent situation where you felt inadequate or struggled. How did you experience God's grace in that moment? Consider how His grace has been evident in your life and has empowered you to overcome challenges. Allow these reflections to deepen your understanding of the transformative power of grace.

Action Step

Identify someone in your life who may need grace and compassion. Reach out to them with an act of kindness or a word of encouragement, extending the same grace that God has shown you. Let this action serve as a reminder of how grace can impact others and bring healing and connection.

Change is Inevitable, but Growth is Optional

Scripture Reading

- ☐ Ecclesiastes 3:1 (NIV): "There is a time for everything, and a season for every activity under the heavens."

- ☐ Romans 12:2 (NIV): "Do not conform to the pattern of this world, but be transformed by the renewing of your mind. Then you will be able to test and approve what God's will is—his good, pleasing and perfect will."

- ☐ Jeremiah 29:11 (NIV): "For I know the plans I have for you,' declares the Lord, 'plans to prosper you and not to harm you, plans to give you hope and a future.'"

Reflection

We Don't Know Who Needs to Hear this, but while change is inevitable, growth is your option!

Change is an intrinsic part of life, a constant and unavoidable force that shapes our experiences and environments. From seasons shifting to personal transitions, change surrounds us continually. While we cannot escape the inevitability of change, how we respond to it—and whether we choose to grow through it—lies within our control.

Ecclesiastes 3:1 reminds us that everything has its season, including periods of change and transition. Understanding that change is part of

God's plan can help us approach it with acceptance rather than resistance. However, how we handle these changes is crucial. The opportunities for growth lie not in the changes themselves but in how we choose to navigate them.

Romans 12:2 calls us to transform rather than conform. In the face of change, we have the option to grow and evolve by renewing our minds. This transformation is a deliberate process that involves aligning our thoughts and actions with God's will rather than simply adapting to external changes. True growth requires us to actively seek God's guidance and embrace the opportunities for spiritual and personal development that come with change.

Prayer

Dear Heavenly Father,

We acknowledge that change is a constant in our lives, often bringing challenges and opportunities. Thank You for being our steadfast anchor in the midst of change. Help us to embrace the changes we face with a heart open to growth and transformation.

Lord, we pray for the strength to navigate transitions with grace and wisdom. When faced with uncertainty or upheaval, guide us in seeking Your will and allowing Your Spirit to renew and transform us. May we not merely adjust to change but use it as a chance to deepen our faith and understanding of You. Teach us to see change as a catalyst for growth rather than a source of fear or discomfort. Help us to remain committed to personal and spiritual development, aligning our lives with Your good, pleasing, and perfect will.

In Jesus' name, we pray.

Amen.

Contemplation

Reflect on a recent or ongoing change in your life. How has this change affected you? Have you found opportunities for growth or transformation during this transition? Consider how your response to change can be guided by your faith and desire for spiritual growth.

Action Step

Identify an area of your life where change is occurring. Rather than resisting or merely adapting to this change, seek ways to actively engage with it for personal and spiritual growth. Spend time in prayer and reflection, asking God how He might be using this change to shape and refine you. Set specific goals for how you can grow through this experience, and seek support from others who can encourage and pray for you in this process.

Blessed and Highly Favored

Scripture Reading

- Luke 12:48 (NIV): "But the one who does not know and does things deserving punishment will be beaten with few blows. From everyone who has been given much, much will be demanded; and from the one who has been entrusted with much, much will be asked."

- Genesis 12:2 (NIV): "I will make you into a great nation, and I will bless you; I will make your name great, and you will be a blessing."

Reflection

We Don't Know Who Needs to Hear this, but with favor comes responsibility!

Being blessed and highly favored is a profound gift from God, but it also comes with a significant responsibility. When God bestows His blessings upon us, He enriches our lives and entrusts us with the duty to use those blessings for His purposes and to serve others.

Luke 12:48 highlights the principle that with great blessings come great responsibilities. The more we are given, the more we are expected to steward those gifts wisely and generously. Whether our blessings are material, relational, or spiritual, we are called to manage them in a way that honors God and serves His kingdom.

Genesis 12:2 exemplifies how God's blessings are intended to be used. When God blessed Abraham, He promised that Abraham would be a blessing to others. This reflects the idea that our blessings are meant to extend beyond ourselves. We are called to be channels of God's grace, using our advantages and resources to bless and uplift others.

Prayer

Heavenly Father,

We thank You for the favor and many blessings You have poured into our lives. We acknowledge that these gifts are from You and that we are entrusted with a great responsibility to use them in ways that honor You and benefit others.

Help us to recognize the weight of our blessings and to steward them with wisdom and grace. Teach us to be generous, using our resources, time, and talents to serve those in need and to further Your kingdom. May we be mindful that our blessings are not just for our own benefit but are meant to be a source of blessing to others.

Lord, guide us in fulfilling the responsibility that comes with being blessed. Let our lives reflect Your love and goodness, and may our actions inspire others to seek You. Empower us to use our blessings to make a positive impact, bringing glory to Your name and drawing others closer to You.

In Jesus' name, we pray.

Amen.

Contemplation

Reflect on the favor and specific blessings that God has given you. How can you use these blessings to serve others and advance His kingdom? Consider how you can be more intentional in your stewardship of these gifts.

Action Step

Identify one area where you can use your blessings to make a difference. It could be through financial support, volunteering your time, or using your skills to help others. Take a concrete step towards fulfilling this responsibility and seek opportunities to be a blessing to those around you. Regularly assess how you manage your blessings and pray for God's guidance in using them effectively.

Be Decisive vs Acting in Haste (Slow Down but Don't Stop)

Scripture Reading

- ☐ Proverbs 4:7 (NIV): "The beginning of wisdom is this: Get wisdom. Though it cost all you have, get understanding."

- ☐ James 1:5 (NIV): "If any of you lacks wisdom, you should ask God, who gives generously to all without finding fault, and it will be given to you."

- ☐ Jeremiah 1:6-8 (NIV): "Alas, Sovereign Lord,' I said, 'I do not know how to speak; I am too young.' But the Lord said to me, 'Do not say, I am too young. You must go to everyone I send you to and say whatever I command you. Do not be afraid of them, for I am with you and will rescue you,' declares the Lord."

Reflection

We Don't Know Who Needs to Hear this, but slow down a bit. Don't stop!

The temptation to act quickly and make hasty decisions can be overwhelming in our fast-paced world. Yet, Scripture encourages us to prioritize wisdom and understanding over impulsivity. Decisiveness, rooted in thoughtful consideration and divine guidance, leads to more prudent and effective outcomes than hasty actions driven by urgency or emotion.

Proverbs 4:7 highlights that wisdom is essential for making sound decisions. Wisdom involves more than just knowledge; it encompasses discernment and understanding, which come from careful reflection and seeking God's guidance. True wisdom may require time and effort but is invaluable and worth pursuing diligently.

James 1:5 offers reassurance that we are not alone in our decision-making process. When we lack wisdom, we can ask God for it. He promises to provide wisdom generously and without reproach, guiding us through the complexities of life. This divine wisdom helps us to act with clarity and purpose rather than rushing into decisions driven by haste or superficial judgments.

Prayer

Heavenly Father,

We come before You, seeking Your guidance and wisdom. In times of decision-making, we often feel the pressure to act quickly, but we recognize the importance of making choices that are rooted in Your truth and understanding. Help us to be decisive, not out of haste, but through thoughtful consideration and prayerful discernment.

Lord, grant us the wisdom to evaluate our options carefully and to seek Your counsel in all matters. May Your Spirit guide our hearts and minds, providing clarity and insight as we navigate the decisions before us. Teach us to value Your perspective over the moment's urgency and trust in Your timing and plan for our lives.

In moments of uncertainty, remind us to turn to You and ask for Your wisdom. May our choices reflect Your will and bring honor to Your name.

In Jesus' name, we pray.

Amen.

Contemplation

Consider a recent decision you made or one that you are currently facing. Reflect on whether it was made in haste or with careful thought and prayer. How might the outcome differ if you had taken more time to seek wisdom and understanding? Allow this reflection to guide you in approaching future decisions with a spirit of discernment.

Action Step

Identify a decision or choice you need to make. Instead of rushing into it, take a deliberate approach by setting aside time for prayer and reflection. Seek God's wisdom through Scripture and counsel from trusted advisors. Commit to waiting until you have a clear sense of direction before proceeding. Use this process to develop a habit of decisiveness grounded in thoughtful consideration rather than haste.

Response vs. Reaction

Scripture Reading

- Proverbs 15:1 (NIV): "A gentle answer turns away wrath, but a harsh word stirs up anger."

- James 1:19 (NIV): "My dear brothers and sisters, take note of this: Everyone should be quick to listen, slow to speak and slow to become angry."

Reflection

We Don't Know Who Needs to Hear this, but learn to respond instead of reacting to everything!

Effective communication is more than just exchanging words; it's about connecting with others meaningfully and respectfully. In today's fast-paced world, where misunderstandings and conflicts are common, the wisdom of Scripture offers timeless guidance on how to communicate effectively and with love.

Proverbs 15:1 reminds us that the tone and intention behind our words matter greatly. A gentle and kind response can de-escalate tensions and foster harmony, whereas a harsh or abrupt response can inflame conflict. This verse calls us to practice gentleness in our interactions, embodying patience and understanding, even in challenging conversations.

James 1:19 underscores the importance of listening before speaking. It teaches us to prioritize active listening, allowing others to fully express their thoughts and feelings before we respond. This approach shows respect and helps us to understand different perspectives, leading to more constructive and empathetic communication.

Prayer

Heavenly Father,

Thank You for the gift of communication and the ability to connect with others through our words and actions. Help us to reflect Your love and grace in our conversations. Grant us the wisdom to choose our words carefully and the patience to listen with an open heart.

Lord, as Your Word instructs, teach us to be quick to listen and slow to speak. May our responses be gentle and filled with understanding, even when faced with disagreement or conflict. Help us embody the peace and kindness of Christ in every interaction, seeking to build others up rather than tearing them down. Guide us in using communication as a tool for unity, compassion, and truth. Let our words be a reflection of Your love, bringing healing and encouragement to those around us. May our conversations be a testament to Your grace and a source of positive change in our relationships and communities.

In Jesus' name, we pray.

Amen.

Contemplation

Take a moment to reflect on your recent conversations. Are there areas where you could apply more patience or gentleness? Consider ways you can actively listen and respond with empathy and love. Commit to practicing these principles in your daily interactions, allowing your communication to reflect your faith and character.

Action Step

Choose one relationship or situation where communication could be improved. Practice active listening and respond with kindness and understanding. Notice how this approach impacts the conversation and the relationship as a whole. Use this experience as a stepping stone to enhance your communication skills and reflect Christ's love in all your interactions.

Finding Peace Amidst Anxiety

Scripture Reflection

- Philippians 4:6-7 (NIV): "Do not be anxious about anything, but in every situation, by prayer and petition, with thanksgiving, present your requests to God. And the peace of God, which transcends all understanding, will guard your hearts and your minds in Christ Jesus."

Reflection

We Don't Know Who Needs to Hear this, but stop unlocking new fears!

It's important to recognize that feeling anxious is a part of the human experience. The disciples themselves faced moments of fear and doubt. Jesus doesn't condemn our anxiety; instead, He invites us to bring it to Him. Are there specific worries weighing on your heart today? Take a moment to name them before God. The verse from Philippians encourages us to present our requests to God through prayer. This is not just a suggestion; it's an invitation to engage in an ongoing conversation with our Creator.

Prayer

Heavenly Father, I come to You with my anxieties and fears. Help me to lay them at Your feet and trust in Your promise of peace. Teach me to be grateful in all circumstances and to seek support from those around me. May Your peace guard my heart and mind today and always.

In Jesus' name, we pray.

Amen.

Contemplation

Anxiety can often feel like an unwelcome companion, creeping into our thoughts and overwhelming our hearts. Feeling isolated and burdened in moments of uncertainty and fear is easy. Yet, as followers of Christ, we are offered a path to peace that transcends our circumstances. Take a moment and consider times when you were the calm in the storm.

Action Step

Set aside time each day for prayer. Speak openly about your worries, and don't hesitate to ask for His guidance and peace.

Vision Without Execution is a Mirage

Scripture Reading

- Proverbs 16:3 (NIV): "Commit to the Lord whatever you do, and he will establish your plans."

- James 2:17 (NIV): "In the same way, faith by itself, if it is not accompanied by action, is dead."

Reflection

We Don't Know Who Needs to Hear this, but vision without execution is hallucinating!

Having a vision is a powerful starting point, but it is only the beginning of the journey. Whether it pertains to personal goals, ministry, or career aspirations, a vision requires more than just dreaming and planning; it demands execution. Without action, even the most compelling vision will remain unrealized.

Proverbs 16:3 encourages us to commit our plans to the Lord. It's not enough to have a vision; we must also dedicate our efforts to God and seek His guidance in the execution. By committing our work to Him, we invite His blessings and direction, ensuring that our efforts are aligned with His will and purposes.

James 2:17 underscores that faith without action is ineffective. This principle applies to our visions as well. It is not enough to merely envision or plan; we must take tangible steps to bring our vision to life. Action is the bridge between a dream and its realization. Our faith in God's guidance and commitment to action make our visions achievable.

Prayer

Dear Heavenly Father,

We thank You for the visions and dreams You place in our hearts. We recognize that having a vision is a gift and a calling, but we also understand that it is not enough alone. Help us to move beyond dreaming and planning to pursuing and executing the plans You have set before us.

Lord, we commit our visions and efforts to You, asking for Your guidance and blessing in every step. Strengthen our resolve to turn our aspirations into action, and grant us the wisdom and perseverance to follow through. May our work reflect Your will and bring glory to Your name.

Guide us in taking practical steps towards our goals and help us to stay focused and diligent. Teach us to balance our vision with execution, trusting that Your hand is upon our efforts and that You will establish our plans according to Your purpose.

In Jesus' name, we pray.

Amen.

Contemplation

Reflect on a vision or goal that you have been contemplating. Have you taken concrete steps towards achieving it, or have you remained in the planning phase? Consider what actions you need to take to move from vision to execution and how you can better align your efforts with God's guidance.

Action Step

Choose one vision or goal that you have been holding onto. Break it into actionable steps and set a timeline for completing each step. Commit these actions to the Lord in prayer, seeking His guidance and blessing. Take the first concrete step towards your goal and continue to seek His direction and strength as you move forward. Track your progress and adjust your plans as needed, always keeping your vision aligned with God's will.

Model the Way

Scripture Reading

- 1 Timothy 4:12 (NIV): "Don't let anyone look down on you because you are young, but set an example for the believers in speech, in conduct, in love, in faith and in purity."

- Matthew 5:14-16 (NIV): "You are the light of the world. A town built on a hill cannot be hidden. Neither do people light a lamp and put it under a bowl. Instead, they put it on its stand, and it gives light to everyone in the house. In the same way, let your light shine before others, that they may see your good deeds and glorify your Father in heaven."

Reflection

We Don't Know Who Needs to Hear this, but practice what you preach!

Modeling the way is about leading by example and reflecting Christ's love and character in our daily lives. Our actions, attitudes, and behaviors serve as a testimony to others and can significantly influence those around us. This concept is deeply rooted in Scripture, which calls us to live in a manner that honors God and inspires others.

1 Timothy 4:12 instructs us to set an example in various aspects of our lives. Regardless of age or status, we are called to be role models in how we speak, act, love, and live out our faith. Our conduct should align with

our beliefs, demonstrating integrity and commitment to God's principles. By setting a positive example, we can encourage others to pursue a similar path of faithfulness and righteousness.

Matthew 5:14-16 emphasizes that as followers of Christ, we are to be lights in the world. Our lives should shine brightly, not for our glory, but to illuminate the path to Christ. Just as a lamp on a stand provides light to everyone in the house, our actions and deeds should reflect the love and goodness of God, leading others to glorify Him.

Prayer

Heavenly Father,

Thank You for calling us to be reflections of Your light in the world. We acknowledge that our lives are a testimony to Your grace and truth. Help us to model the way in speech, conduct, love, faith, and purity so that others may see Your character in us.

Lord, guide us in living out our faith authentically so that our actions reflect Your love and righteousness. Strengthen us to be examples of Your light in all we do, allowing Your presence to shine through us. Let our good deeds and sincere love draw others to You and bring glory to Your name.

Help us to remember that our influence extends beyond our immediate circle. May our lives be a beacon of hope and encouragement, pointing others to the truth of Your Word. Teach us to live in a way that honors You and inspires others to follow You more closely.

In Jesus' name, we pray.

Amen.

Contemplation

Consider how you can model the way in your daily interactions. Can you reflect Christ's love and character more clearly in specific areas? Reflect on the impact of your actions and how they might influence those around you.

Action Step

Identify one area of your life where you want to be a stronger role model. This could be in your speech, conduct, relationship approach, or integrity. Set a specific goal for how you will embody Christ's example in this area and seek accountability from a trusted friend or mentor. Regularly evaluate your progress and pray for God's strength to remain a faithful example to others.

Weapons May Form, but They Won't Succeed

Scripture

- Isaiah 54:17 (NIV): "No weapon forged against you will prevail, and you will refute every tongue that accuses you. This is the heritage of the servants of the Lord, and this is their vindication from me," declares the Lord.

Reflection

We Don't Know Who Needs to Hear this, but God doesn't play about you!

In our journey through life, we often face challenges that seem insurmountable. Whether it's a physical ailment, emotional turmoil, financial strain, or conflict in relationships, it can feel as though we are under siege. The promise in Isaiah 54:17 is a powerful reminder of God's protection and sovereignty over our lives.

When the scripture says, "No weapon formed against you shall prosper," it is not an assurance that weapons will never be formed but that they will not succeed in their intended harm. The "weapons" could be anything from negative thoughts and harmful words to more tangible threats and adversities. God acknowledges their existence but promises their failure in harming us.

1. *Embrace God's Protection:* This verse is a declaration of divine protection. It means that no matter what we face, God is our shield. Reflect on times when you felt under attack and see how God has provided a way through or delivered you from danger. Embracing this truth encourages faith and trust in God's unfailing protection.

2. *Stand Firm in Faith*: Refuting every tongue that accuses you is not merely about defending ourselves with our words but standing firm in our identity in Christ. When accusations or criticisms come your way, remember that your worth and identity are rooted in God's love and promises. Stand on His truth rather than the lies that may be spoken against you.

3. *Claim Your Heritage:* The promise of vindication and protection is part of our heritage as servants of the Lord. This heritage is not just a distant promise but a present reality. Understanding that you are part of God's family, with all its privileges and protections, should bolster your confidence and hope. It is a reminder of the covenant relationship you have with your Creator.

4. *Pray with Confidence*: When facing challenges, approach God in prayer with the confidence that He will protect and uphold you. Ask for His strength to overcome difficulties and for His wisdom to navigate through them. Trust that He will fight for you, as the verse assures, and that His purposes will prevail over any schemes against you.

Prayer

Heavenly Father,

I thank You for the promise that no weapon formed against me shall prosper. When faced with trials and attacks, help me remember that You are my protector and that nothing can separate me from Your love. Strengthen my faith and help me to stand firm in Your truth. May I find peace in Your assurance and boldly live out the identity You have given me. Thank You for Your unending faithfulness and for being my refuge and fortress.

In Jesus' name, we pray.

Amen.

Contemplation

As you go through today, reflect on the areas where you feel vulnerable or under attack. Remember that God's promise covers every aspect of your life. Meditate on His protection and allow His peace to reign in your heart. Trust that His plans for you are good and that He works all things together for your good.

Action

Embrace the promise of Isaiah 54:17 by internalizing the assurance that no weapon formed against you will prosper, and your righteousness is from the Lord. Begin each day with an affirmation of faith, such as, "I am protected, and my righteousness comes from the Lord." Identify any fears or judgments you face, consciously releasing and replacing them with positive affirmations about your worth and purpose. Pray regularly for strength and guidance to navigate challenges and support others by sharing this message of hope and protection, encouraging those who may also need reassurance in trying times.

Crushing Self-Doubt

Scripture Reading

- Jeremiah 29:11 (NIV): "For I know the plans I have for you," declares the Lord, "plans to prosper you and not to harm you, plans to give you hope and a future."

Reflection

We Don't Know Who Needs to Hear this, but you are amazing!

Self-doubt can make us forget our purpose and paralyze us with fear of the unknown. Jeremiah 29:11 is a powerful reminder that God has a unique plan for each of us. His plans include hope and a prosperous future. When we understand that our lives are part of a divine blueprint, the grip of self-doubt starts to loosen. Trust that God's vision for your life goes beyond your current insecurities.

Prayer

Lord, I struggle with thoughts that undermine my worth and abilities. Help me to remember that You have great plans for my life. Replace my self-doubt with Your confidence and guide me according to Your will.

In Jesus' name, we pray.

Amen.

Contemplation

Self-doubt is like an unwelcome guest that often overstays its welcome, making you second-guess your decisions, potential, and worth. Think about those moments when doubt seemed to flood your mind. What triggered those feelings? Perhaps it was a challenging project at work, a relationship struggle, or stepping out of your comfort zone. How did those doubts affect your actions and mindset? Imagine handing over your worries to God, knowing He has meticulously crafted a plan for your future—a plan filled with hope. Picture every step you take as guided by His hand, infused with His wisdom and purpose. When faced with doubt, visualizing this divine support can alter your mental landscape, transforming fear into faith and uncertainty into unwavering confidence.

Action Step

Identify one area in your life where self-doubt regularly appears. Commit to speaking positivity over that area daily, using Jeremiah 29:11 as a foundational truth. Write it on a sticky note and place it where you'll see it—your bathroom mirror, desk, or bedside table. Let this constant reminder of God's plan help you speak the truth over your doubt.

Embracing Your Worth

Scripture Reading

- Psalm 139:14 (NIV): "I praise you because I am fearfully and wonderfully made; your works are wonderful, I know that full well."

Reflection

We Don't Know Who Needs to Hear this, but you are worthy!

We often struggle with feelings of inadequacy and wonder if we measure up. Psalm 139:14 affirms that you are fearfully and wonderfully made. God took His time with you, crafting each detail with intention and love. Embrace the wonderful creation that you are, knowing that you hold extraordinary value.

Prayer

Lord, thank You for creating me with such care and love. Help me to see myself through Your eyes and to embrace my worth fully. Give me confidence in the unique person You have made me to be.

In Jesus' name, we pray.

Amen.

Contemplation

Take a moment to think about how you view yourself. Are you kind to yourself, or do you focus on flaws and shortcomings? Imagine looking at yourself through God's eyes. He sees your beauty, your strengths, and the potential He placed inside you. When you start to align your self-view with God's perspective, self-doubt begins to shift into self-acceptance. Contemplate the truth that you are wonderfully made; this isn't just a fleeting compliment but an eternal fact. Begin to let this truth sink into your heart and mind. Consider keeping a journal where you jot down the qualities you love about yourself, the strengths you noticed today, and the characteristics friends and family commonly praise. Reflecting on these can help solidify your understanding of your inherent worth.

Action Step

Write down three qualities you admire about yourself and keep them in your purse, wallet, or phone. Review these qualities every morning to remind yourself of your God-given worth.

Trusting God's Timing

Scripture Reading

- Ecclesiastes 3:1 (NIV): "There is a time for everything; and a season for every activity under the heavens."

Reflection

We Don't Know Who Needs to Hear this, but timing matters!

In a world where instant gratification is often the norm, remaining patient and trusting God's timing can be challenging. Ecclesiastes 3:1 reminds us that everything happens in its perfect season. Trusting in God's timetable, even when it doesn't align with our desires, can bring immense peace and assurance.

Prayer

Dear Lord, teach me to trust Your timing in every area of my life. Help me remain patient and faithful, believing You know what is best for me. Guide my steps and grant me the wisdom to align my timing with Yours.

In Jesus' name, we pray.

Amen.

Contemplation

Consider how often you find yourself impatient or anxious about the future. Does waiting make you doubt whether things will happen at all? Trusting God's timing requires a shift in perspective. It means believing He sees the bigger picture and knows the optimal moment for each event in your life. Think about the times when delays seemed to be a setup for something greater. For instance, maybe a job you wanted didn't come through but later led you to a better opportunity. Reflect on these experiences and draw strength from them. When you fully grasp that there is a season for everything, it can ease the urgency and fear that often accompany waiting, allowing you to rest in God's perfect timing.

Action Step

Identify an area in your life where you find yourself impatient. Make a conscious decision to surrender it to God's timing. When that impatience rises, remind yourself of Ecclesiastes 3:1 and declare it over your situation.

Overcoming Anxiety

Scripture Reading

- Philippians 4:6-7 (NIV): "Do not be anxious about anything, but in every situation, by prayer and petition, with thanksgiving, present your requests to God. And the peace of God, which transcends all understanding, will guard your hearts and your minds in Christ Jesus."

Reflection

We Don't Know Who Needs to Hear this, but you've got this!

Anxiety can cripple our peace and joy. Philippians 4:6-7 offers a practical solution: bring your worries to God through prayer and thanksgiving. Instead of being overwhelmed, turn your anxiety into an opportunity to connect with God and lean on His peace.

Prayer

Heavenly Father, I bring my anxieties to You today. Help me to lay them at Your feet and trust that You are in control. Fill my heart with Your peace that surpasses all understanding.

In Jesus' name, we pray.

Amen.

Contemplation

Think about your usual response to anxiety. Do you tend to dwell on what-ifs and worst-case scenarios? What if you saw anxiety as an invitation to prayer? Each worry is a chance to bring your concerns before God and exchange them for His peace. Imagine releasing every anxious thought like a balloon, watching each one drift up to God. Understand that His peace is not a mere absence of worry but a profound assurance that guards your heart and mind amidst turmoil. Regularly redirecting anxious thoughts to prayer can reshape your reaction, allowing peace to become your default state.

Action Step

Next time you feel anxious, write down your specific worries and transform them into prayers. Keep adding to your prayer list and note when and how God provides peace and solutions.

Building Strong Relationships

Scripture Reading

- 1 Corinthians 13:4-7 (NIV): "Love is patient, love is kind. It does not envy, it does not boast, it is not proud. It does not dishonor others, it is not self-seeking, it is not easily angered, it keeps no record of wrongs. Love does not delight in evil but rejoices with the truth. It always protects, always trusts, always hopes, always perseveres."

Reflection

We Don't Know Who Needs to Hear this, but how you show love to others reflects how you love yourself!

Relationships can be challenging, but 1 Corinthians 13:4-7 provides a blueprint for how to love others effectively. Cultivating patience, kindness, and humility while forgiving and trusting others creates deeper connections and fosters genuine relationships.

Prayer

Lord, teach me how to love others as You love me. Help me to be patient, kind, and humble, always seeking the best in others. Strengthen my relationships through Your enduring love.

In Jesus' name, we pray.

Amen.

Contemplation

Focus on your current relationships. Which aspects of love from 1 Corinthians 13 do you find easy? Which are more challenging? Think about how embodying these traits can transform your interactions. True love requires effort and intentionality. Reflecting on God's love for us—unconditional and unwavering—can provide the strength needed to exhibit this kind of love to others. Realize that loving well isn't just about grand gestures; it's also about consistent, everyday actions and attitudes. Small acts of kindness, a gentle word, or patience during a minor disagreement can go a long way in nurturing long-lasting relationships.

Action Step

Choose one relationship to focus on this week. Make a conscious effort to practice patience, kindness, or forgiveness in your interactions with this person.

Finding Joy in the Journey

Scripture Reading

☐ James 1:2-3 (NIV): "Consider it pure joy, my brothers and sisters, whenever you face trials of many kinds, because you know that the testing of your faith produces perseverance."

Reflection

We Don't Know Who Needs to Hear this, but your joy cannot be snatched!

Life's challenges can feel overwhelming, but James 1:2-3 encourages us to view them as opportunities for growth. Trials are chances to develop perseverance and maturity in our faith. Finding joy in the journey means recognizing the value in each experience, even the difficult ones.

Prayer

God, thank You for the trials that strengthen my faith. Help me to find joy in every part of my journey, knowing that each challenge brings me closer to You. Please grant me the perseverance to keep moving forward.

In Jesus' name, we pray.

Amen.

Contemplation

Reflect on a recent trial you've faced. How did it shape you? What did you learn about yourself and your faith? Consider how choosing to find joy in the midst of it could have changed your perspective. Trials are tough, but they often bring unseen growth. Think about the lessons learned, the strength gained, and the deeper reliance on God that emerged from those difficulties.

Embrace the idea that God is more interested in your character than in making your life easy. Use every challenge as a stepping stone toward developing deeper faith and perseverance.

Action Step

List three challenges you currently face and describe how each could build your faith and character. Pray for these areas, asking God to reveal His purpose and joy through them.

Forgiveness Sets You Free

Scripture Reading

- Ephesians 4:32 (NIV): "Be kind and compassionate to one another, forgiving each other, just as in Christ God forgave you."

Reflection

We Don't Know Who Needs to Hear this, but forgiveness is not for them; it's for you!

Holding on to grudges or past hurts can weigh us down. Ephesians 4:32 calls us to forgive others as Christ has forgiven us. True forgiveness can set both parties free, fostering healing and peace.

Prayer

Father, help me to forgive as You have forgiven me. Release me from the burden of grudges and past hurts. Fill my heart with kindness and compassion, allowing Your love to heal and restore.

In Jesus' name, we pray.

Amen.

Contemplation

Take a moment to identify any lingering grudges you hold. Who do you struggle to forgive, and why? Reflect on how holding onto these feelings impacts you. Holding onto resentment is like walking around with a heavy backpack; it only burdens you. God understands the pain of betrayal and mistreatment, but He still offers grace and forgiveness to us. Contemplate the freedom that comes with letting go of past hurts. Offering forgiveness doesn't mean excusing the wrong but choosing to release its hold on you. It's a gift of freedom to yourself as much as to others.

Action Step

To embody the teachings of Ephesians 4:32, actively practice kindness and compassion in your daily interactions by being attentive and thoughtful towards others. Make a conscious effort to let go of grudges and forgive those who have hurt you, just as God forgave you through Christ. Begin by doing a simple act of kindness each day, whether offering a compliment, lending a helping hand, or listening to someone who needs support. Reflect on your emotions and address any lingering bitterness by focusing on empathy and understanding. Engage in prayer or meditation to seek strength and guidance in cultivating a forgiving heart, aiming to create a more harmonious and loving environment for yourself and those around you.

Trusting God's Plan

Scripture Reading

- Proverbs 3:5-6 (NIV): "Trust in the Lord with all your heart and lean not on your own understanding; in all your ways submit to Him, and He will make your paths straight."

Reflection

We Don't Know Who Needs to Hear this, but God has it all under control!

Trusting in God's plan can be challenging, especially when life doesn't go as expected. Proverbs 3:5-6 encourages us to trust God wholeheartedly, knowing He sees the bigger picture. Submitting to His guidance ensures that He will direct our paths.

Prayer

Heavenly Father, I submit my plans to You. Help me to trust Your wisdom and guidance, even when I don't understand it. Lead me on the right path and give me the courage to follow You.

In Jesus' name, we pray.

Amen.

Contemplation

Think about areas where you struggle to trust God's plan. Is it your career, relationships, or future? Why is surrendering control difficult for you?

Trusting God involves releasing our need for certainty and control. Reflect on past moments when you relied on your understanding and how it turned out compared to times you placed your trust in God. Think of God as a loving parent guiding you where, even unseen, His plans are made in your best interest. Surrendering isn't about resigning to fate but embracing faith.

Understand that God's omniscient view surpasses our limited perspective.

Action Step

Write down your biggest concerns and uncertainties. Beside each, jot a prayer of surrender, asking God to guide you and help you trust His plan.

Embracing Your Identity in Christ

Scripture Reading

- ☐ Galatians 2:20 (NIV): "I have been crucified with Christ and I no longer live, but Christ lives in me. The life I now live in the body, I live by faith in the Son of God, who loved me and gave himself for me."

Reflection

We Don't Know Who Needs to Hear this, but you are a child of the King…now act like it!

Our identity in Christ transforms how we see ourselves and how we live. Embracing that we are new creations in Him, we can live out our faith confidently, knowing that Christ's power and love define who we are.

Prayer

Lord Jesus, thank You for giving me a new identity in You. Help me live out this truth daily, remembering that I am loved, redeemed, and empowered by Your Spirit. May my life reflect the reality of Christ within me.

In Jesus' name, we pray.

Amen.

Contemplation

Reflect on how you see yourself. Are there previous labels or mistakes that still shape your identity? Consider the difference between earthly identity and heavenly identity. Earthly identity might be flawed and inconsistent, but you are a beloved child of God, redeemed and renewed in Christ. Ponder the immense love that Christ has for you that He dwells within you, shaping your character, choices, and purpose. Accepting this, you gain a sense of stability and value that transcends human measures.

Action Step

Create a personal affirmation statement based on your identity in Christ. Begin each day by declaring this truth over yourself, allowing it to guide your actions and decisions.

Living a Life of Generosity

Scripture Reading

- 2 Corinthians 9:7 (NIV): "Each of you should give what you have decided in your heart to give, not reluctantly or under compulsion, for God loves a cheerful giver."

Reflection

We Don't Know Who Needs to Hear this, but an unselfish heart can change someone's day!

Generosity goes beyond material wealth; it encompasses our time, talents, and love. 2 Corinthians 9:7 calls us to give cheerfully and willingly. When we embrace a lifestyle of generosity, we reflect God's heart and impact others positively.

Prayer

Lord, cultivate a generous spirit within me. Help me to give cheerfully and willingly, sharing my resources, time, and love as acts of worship to You. Let my generosity be a testament to Your goodness.

In Jesus' name, we pray.

Amen.

Contemplation

Think about your attitude towards giving. Do you give out of obligation or find joy in it? What are some non-material ways you can be generous? Generosity, rooted in love, brings profound joy. It's an expression of God's abundant provision in our lives. Reflect on how God has been generous with you in countless ways and how this abundance inspires the desire to share with others. True generosity stems from understanding that everything we have is a gift from God, meant to be shared to enrich the lives of others.

Action Step

This week, identify a way to be generous—volunteer your time, offer a listening ear, or share resources with someone in need. Do it with a cheerful heart, and note how it impacts you and those around you.

Strength in Weakness

Scripture Reading

- 2 Corinthians 12:9-10 (NIV): "But He said to me, 'My grace is sufficient for you, for My power is made perfect in weakness.' Therefore, I will boast all the more gladly about my weaknesses, so that Christ's power may rest on me. That is why, for Christ's sake, I delight in weaknesses, in insults, in hardships, in persecutions, in difficulties. For when I am weak, then I am strong."

Reflection

We Don't Know Who Needs to Hear this, but God is strong enough for both of you!

Acknowledging our weaknesses allows God's power to work through us. 2 Corinthians 12:9-10 teaches that God's grace is sufficient, and His strength is made perfect in our weakness. Embracing our vulnerabilities can enable us to experience Christ's power more fully.

Prayer

Father, remind me that Your grace is all I need. In my moments of weakness, show me Your strength. Help me to trust that my limitations are opportunities for Your power to manifest.

In Jesus' name, we pray.

Amen.

Contemplation

Reflect on where you feel weak or insufficient. How does it affect your trust in God and your self-perception? Consider the paradox of strength in weakness. God's power shines most clearly through our vulnerabilities because it's then that we rely entirely on Him. Ponder on biblical figures like Paul, Moses, and David, who recognized their limitations yet were used mightily by God. Embracing your weaknesses opens the door to extraordinary experiences of God's strength. Your imperfections become the canvas on which God's perfect strength paints masterpieces.

Action Step

To internalize the message of 2 Corinthians 12:9-10, embrace your weaknesses and challenges as opportunities for God's power to manifest in your life. Start by acknowledging and accepting your limitations rather than hiding or being ashamed of them. When faced with difficulties, pray or meditate to seek God's grace and strength to carry you through. Practice humility by being open about your struggles with trusted friends or loved ones, allowing them to support you and witness God's work in your life. Celebrate progress and victories, big or small, recognizing that these are made possible through divine strength. Shift your focus from self-reliance to faith, trusting that God's power is perfected in your moments of weakness and will lead you to true strength.

Finding Hope in Brokenness

Scripture Reading

- Psalm 34:18 (NIV): "The Lord is close to the brokenhearted and saves those who are crushed in spirit."

Reflection

We Don't Know Who Needs to Hear this, but God specializes in putting broken pieces back together!

Life can break our hearts in many ways—through disappointment, loss, or personal failure. Psalm 34:18 is a comforting reminder that God is near in those moments of brokenness. He doesn't abandon us but draws close to us, offering comfort and salvation when we feel most crushed.

Prayer

Dear Lord, draw near to me in my moments of heartache and brokenness. Help me to feel Your comforting presence and remind me that You are always close. Heal my heart and make me whole again with Your love.

In Jesus' name, we pray.

Amen.

Contemplation

When facing brokenness, it's easy to feel isolated and think you must face it alone. But God's promise in Psalm 34:18 reassures you that He is intimately aware of your pain and stands with you through it. Reflect on times when you felt God's presence in your lowest moments. Instead of pushing through alone, think about how you can lean into God's support. Imagine His arms wrapping around you, providing solace and strength. Consider sharing your struggles with a supportive community, allowing them to be God's hands and feet in your time of need.

Action Step

Spend some quiet time in prayer or meditation, inviting God to speak to your broken places. Journal your feelings and any insights you receive. Reach out to someone you trust to talk about your struggles; their support can serve as a tangible expression of God's love and nearness.

Embracing Healing Through Vulnerability

Scripture Reading

☐ James 5:16 (NIV): "Therefore confess your sins to each other and pray for each other so that you may be healed. The prayer of a righteous person is powerful and effective."

Reflection

We Don't Know Who Needs to Hear this, but you're not in this by yourself!

James 5:16 highlights the value of being open and honest about our struggles. Healing often requires courage to be vulnerable. By sharing our brokenness with others, we receive support and experience powerful spiritual healing through collective prayer and accountability.

Prayer

Lord, grant me the courage to be vulnerable and transparent with my struggles. Help me to trust in the healing power of prayer and community. Lead me to the right people with whom I can share openly. May Your strength be made perfect in my weakness.

In Jesus' name, we pray.

Amen.

Contemplation

Vulnerability can be scary because it exposes parts of ourselves we prefer to keep hidden. However, true healing often begins with bravely revealing our wounds to those we trust. Contemplate the walls you've built to guard your hurt; are they keeping others out, or you locked in? Reflect on past instances where sharing your pain led to support and recovery. Understand that vulnerability is not a sign of weakness but a courageous step toward wholeness. Think of how Jesus displayed vulnerability and allowed others to share in His suffering and mission.

Action Step

Identify one trusted person in your life with whom you can share a current struggle. Open up to them and invite them to pray with you, embracing the process of mutual support and healing.

Strengthened by Grace

Scripture Reading

- 2 Corinthians 12:9-10 (NIV): "But He said to me, 'My grace is sufficient for you, for My power is made perfect in weakness.' Therefore, I will boast all the more gladly about my weaknesses, so that Christ's power may rest on me. That is why, for Christ's sake, I delight in weaknesses, in insults, in hardships, in persecutions, in difficulties. For when I am weak, then I am strong."

Reflection

We Don't Know Who Needs to Hear this, but you're not in this alone!

Recognizing our limitations can be disheartening, but it's precisely in our weaknesses that God's grace shines brightest. 2 Corinthians 12:9-10 reminds us that God's grace is not only enough but perfect. Our brokenness becomes the space where His divine power operates most effectively.

Prayer

Gracious Father, I acknowledge my weaknesses and limitations. Let Your grace fill those gaps and transform my brokenness into a testament of Your power. Remind me daily that Your strength is perfected in my weakness.

In Jesus' name, we pray.

Amen.

Contemplation

Reflect on the areas where you feel most weak or inadequately equipped. How do these feelings affect your daily life and outlook? Consider the beauty of God's grace—it's not about making you self-sufficient but making His power evident through you. Your vulnerabilities are not failings; they're opportunities for God to demonstrate His sufficiency. Think about people or situations where you saw divine strength manifest in human weakness. Ponder how embracing your weaknesses can become a source of glory and reliance on God's powerful grace.

Action Step

List your perceived weaknesses and ask God to show you how His grace can transform them. Share one of these areas with someone, letting them know how God's grace is helping you through it.

Beauty from Ashes: Transforming Brokenness into Beauty

Scripture Reading

- ☐ Isaiah 61:3 (NIV): "And provide for those who grieve in Zion—to bestow on them a crown of beauty instead of ashes, the oil of joy instead of mourning, and a garment of praise instead of a spirit of despair. They will be called oaks of righteousness, a planting of the Lord for the display of his splendor."

Reflection

We Don't Know Who Needs to Hear this, but there's a blessing on the other side of this!

Isaiah 61:3 offers a powerful image of transformation—beauty emerging from ashes. God's redemptive power can turn our brokenness, grief, and despair into something beautiful. This scripture reassures us that God can create something profoundly beautiful and joyous out of our deepest sorrows.

Prayer

Lord, in my brokenness and grief, exchange my ashes for Your beauty. Fill my heart with joy and my life with praise, even in the darkest moments. Show me the beauty You are creating from my pain.

In Jesus' name, we pray.

Amen.

Contemplation

Think of times when you felt surrounded by ashes, mourning, or despair. How did you see God's hand at work, subtly or boldly, during those times? The metaphor of turning ashes into beauty symbolizes hope, renewal, and resurrection. Reflect on God's promise to redeem every broken situation, not necessarily by removing the pain but by transforming it into a source of future strength and beauty. Contemplate how God's transformative power has turned past hardships into blessings. Understanding this central theme in the Christian walk—that God brings new life out of suffering—invites you to trust Him deeply, even amid current struggles.

Action Step

Reflect on a past hardship and identify the beauty that emerged from the ashes. Share this story with someone who might need encouragement that God can transform their situation, too.

Uplifted by God's Promises

Scripture Reading

☐ Psalm 55:22 (NIV): "Cast your cares on the Lord and e will sustain you; He will never let the righteous be shaken."

Reflection

We Don't Know Who Needs to Hear this, but God is working behind the scenes!

Life often throws curveballs that can leave us feeling overwhelmed and needing support. Psalm 55:22 reminds us to place our burdens on the Lord. His promises assure us that He will uphold us, and we won't be shaken by adversities when we rely on Him.

Prayer

Dear God, help me to cast my cares upon You. Teach me to lean on Your promises, knowing that You will sustain me through whatever challenges lie ahead. Strengthen my faith to trust that You will never let me be shaken.

In Jesus' name, we pray.

Amen.

Contemplation

Think about the areas in your life where you're carrying too much on your own. It could be work stress, family issues, or personal challenges. How often do you turn to God with these concerns? Reflect on the promise that the Lord will sustain you. It doesn't mean life becomes trouble-free, but you're not alone in facing those troubles. You can release the weight of your burdens and trust in God's enduring strength. Consider times when you felt upheld by His promise, even when situations were tough. Visualize the act of casting your concerns onto Him, knowing that His arms are strong and His care for you is infinite.

Action Step

Take a moment to write down your current worries. In prayer, lift each one to God, imagining yourself placing them into His capable hands. Commit to revisiting this list at the end of the week to see how He has been working in these areas.

Strength Through Community

Scripture Reading

- ☐ Hebrews 10:24-25 (NIV): "And let us consider how we may spur one another on toward love and good deeds, not giving up meeting together, as some are in the habit of doing, but encouraging one another—and all the more as you see the Day approaching."

Reflection

We Don't Know Who Needs to Hear this, but you are your brother's keeper!

Hebrews 10:24-25 emphasizes the importance of community and mutual encouragement. In the context of fellowship, we find the strength to continue performing good deeds and showing love. Isolation can diminish our spirit, but regular interaction with a supportive community uplifts and energizes us.

Prayer

Lord, thank You for the gift of community. Help me to be a source of encouragement and support to others, and allow me to receive the same when needed. Encourage us to meet together in Your name, spurring one another toward love and good deeds.

In Jesus' name, we pray.

Amen.

Contemplation

Reflect on the role of community in your life. Do you regularly engage with a group that encourages your spiritual and personal growth? Loneliness can lead to discouragement, but shared faith can help you stand firm. Contemplate the ways you can both give and receive encouragement within your community. Think about past experiences where a group of friends or a faith community helped you through a tough time or inspired you to take positive action. In these supportive networks, we often find the strength and motivation to keep going, motivated by collective faith and love.

Action Step

Reach out to someone in your community this week. It could be a friend, family member, or fellow believer. Spend time encouraging them through a coffee meet-up, a call, or a message reminding them of God's love and promises.

Renewed by God's Word

Scripture Reading

- ☐ Joshua 1:9 (NIV): "Have I not commanded you? Be strong and courageous. Do not be afraid; do not be discouraged, for the Lord your God will be with you wherever you go."

Reflection

We Don't Know Who Needs to Hear this, but God is right there with you every step of the way!

Facing new challenges can often bring fear and discouragement. In Joshua 1:9, God commands strength and courage, assuring that His presence will accompany us wherever we go. Holding on to these words can renew our spirit and encourage us in every circumstance.

Prayer

Heavenly Father, instill in me the courage and strength You commanded Joshua. Remind me that Your presence is always with me, guiding and protecting me through all life's journeys. Remove my fears and help me walk boldly in Your promises.

In Jesus' name, we pray.

Amen.

Contemplation

Reflect on situations where fear and discouragement have held you back. How often do you remember God's promises in Joshua 1:9 when you face significant changes or challenges? Taking God at His word can transform your outlook, turning fear into faith and discouragement into determination. Imagine God speaking these words directly to you, infusing you with the courage needed to take your next steps. Whether starting a new job, moving to a new city, or confronting a tough decision, knowing God is with you allows you to approach each situation with newfound strength and confidence.

Action Step

Write down Joshua 1:9 and place it somewhere visible, such as on your bathroom mirror or fridge. Reflect on it daily, especially when facing a new or daunting task. Let this verse guide your actions and decisions throughout the week.

Restoration Through Rest

Scripture Reading

☐ Matthew 11:28 (NIV): "Come to me, all you who are weary and burdened, and I will give you rest."

Reflection

We Don't Know Who Needs to Hear this, but reach out to God; you'll find the peace you need!

Jesus invites those weary and burdened to find rest in Him—an essential element for encouragement and renewal. This rest is not just physical but also a deep, soul-refreshing rest that rejuvenates our spirit. Amid our busy lives, taking time to rest in His presence restores our strength.

Prayer

Jesus, I come to You with my weariness and burdens. Please grant me the rest You promise. Help me to find moments of peace and rejuvenation in Your presence. Fill my heart with Your comforting and renewing spirit.

In Jesus' name, we pray.

Amen.

Contemplation

Consider the moments when you've felt truly rested—not just after a good night's sleep, but a profound sense of peace and restoration. How often do you allow yourself to slow down and rest in Jesus' presence? Today's culture prizes constant productivity, sometimes at the cost of our well-being. Reflect on Jesus' invitation to rest. It's not a sign of weakness but an essential pause that refreshes your soul and restores your energy. Consider how incorporating regular resting periods in God's presence can positively impact your mental, emotional, and spiritual health, providing a wellspring of encouragement that sustains you throughout your living.

Action Step

Schedule a specific time this week to rest in the Lord. It could be a half-hour to pray, meditate on scripture, or simply sit quietly and focus on God's presence. Commit to making this a regular practice in your life.

Standing on Business, God's Business

Scripture Reading

- Jeremiah 29:11 (NIV): "For I know the plans I have for you, declares the Lord, plans to prosper you and not to harm you, plans to give you hope and a future."

Reflection

We Don't Know Who Needs to Hear this, but remember God has a plan specifically for you!

In a world that often seems unpredictable, Jeremiah 29:11 provides a comforting reminder that God has a plan for each of us. These plans are designed to bring hope and a promising future. When we remember that our steps are guided by His divine plan, we can confidently prepare for what lies ahead.

Prayer

Dear Lord, thank You for having a plan for my life. Help me trust in Your guidance and find peace in knowing that You have a hopeful future laid out for me. Give me the wisdom and courage to follow Your path.

In Jesus' name, we pray.

Amen.

Contemplation

Think about the plans or ambitions you have for your life. Are they aligned with the trust that God has a purposeful blueprint for you? Often, we may question our direction or feel uncertain about our choices, but God's assurance in Jeremiah 29:11 invites us into a state of trust. Reflect on times when you felt divinely guided, when things seemingly fell into place, even when circumstances were tricky. Consider what it means to truly rest, knowing that a greater plan is at work. This doesn't remove the effort on our part but transforms our preparation into an act of faith, knowing that as we make plans, they are interwoven with God's greater scheme for our prosperity and hope.

Action Step

Write down a specific goal or decision you're currently contemplating. Pray for guidance and ask God to show you His plan for this area of your life. Keep this goal in your prayers, and remain open to His direction.

Be Prepared for Your Purpose

Scripture Reading

- 2 Timothy 3:16-17 (NIV): "All Scripture is God-breathed and is useful for teaching, rebuking, correcting, and training in righteousness, so that the servant of God may be thoroughly equipped for every good work."

Reflection

We Don't Know Who Needs to Hear this, but remember, it's what He said...not what they said!

The Bible equips us with the knowledge and moral framework needed for righteous living and good works. Through its teachings, we are prepared to handle life's challenges and opportunities. It is vital to immerse ourselves in Scripture to be fully equipped for the good works God sets before us.

Prayer

Heavenly Father, thank You for Your word, which equips me for every good work. Help me to diligently study the Scripture and to apply its truths in my life. Use it to prepare me for the purposes You have planned.

In Jesus' name, we pray.

Amen.

Contemplation

Reflect on how often you turn to Scripture when preparing for life's various facets like work, relationships, or day-to-day encounters. The Bible isn't just a book of stories but a manual crafted for your spiritual and practical readiness. How does immersing yourself in God's word shape your decisions and actions? Contemplate the areas where you've noticed God's hand guiding you through Biblical precepts, furnishing you with wisdom and strength. Recognize that nurturing a habit of regular Scripture Reading transforms your preparation for life's tasks from mere capability to thorough equipping for service and righteousness, aligning your actions with God's divine will.

Action Step

Choose a Bible reading plan that fits into your daily routine. Commit to spending at least 10 minutes reading and reflecting on Scripture each day, allowing God to equip you through His word.

Strength in Waiting

Scripture Reading

- Isaiah 40:31 (NIV): "But those who hope in the Lord will renew their strength. They will soar on wings like eagles; they will run and not grow weary, they will walk and not be faint."

Reflection

We Don't Know Who Needs to Hear this, but this earthly life is short; never stop chasing your dreams!

Waiting on the Lord can feel challenging, especially in a culture that values instant results. Isaiah 40:31 assures us that those who place their hope in God will find renewed strength. In this waiting period, we are being prepared to soar to new heights, run life's race with endurance, and walk without fainting.

Prayer

Lord, teach me to wait upon You with eagerness and patience. Renew my strength during times of waiting and preparation. Help me to trust that Your timing is perfect and that You are preparing me for greater things.

In Jesus' name, we pray.

Amen.

Contemplation

Think about seasons in your life where waiting was difficult. How did these periods prepare you for the next steps in your journey? Isaiah 40:31 speaks volumes about the transformative power of waiting on God. It's not a stagnant time but one where your heart and spirit are being fortified. Contemplate the unique ways God renews your strength during these times. Are you growing more patient, more steadfast, or more hopeful? Reflect on the reassurance that waiting on God leads to strength that defies human understanding, enabling you to traverse life's ups and downs with divine support and resilience. How might viewing waiting as a preparation period, rather than mere delay, change your perspective on current circumstances?

Action Step

Identify an area in your life where you are currently waiting for something to happen. Instead of focusing on the wait, focus on how you can prepare yourself during this time. Engage in prayer, read books, or take courses related to this area, allowing God to strengthen and prepare you.

Going Through the Fire

Scripture Reading

- 1 Peter 1:6-7 (NIV): "In all this you greatly rejoice, though now for a little while you may have had to suffer grief in all kinds of trials. These have come so that the proven genuineness of your faith—of greater worth than gold, which perishes even though refined by fire—may result in praise, glory, and honor when Jesus Christ is revealed."

Reflection

We Don't Know Who Needs to Hear this, but remember, when life throws curveballs, never stop swinging!

Going through tough times can often feel overwhelming and endless. As 1 Peter 1:6-7 reminds us, our trials have a purpose—they refine our faith, making it more precious than gold. While the process may be painful, the outcome is a more robust, purer faith that shines brightly for God's glory.

Prayer

Dear Lord, when I face trials, help me to remember their role in refining my faith. Please give me the strength to endure the challenges and to see them as opportunities for growth and transformation. Refine me so that my faith becomes genuine and brings glory to You.

In Jesus' name, we pray.

Amen.

Contemplation

Reflect on the trials you are currently facing or have faced in the past. Think about how these experiences have shaped and strengthened your faith. Our true character and reliance on God often emerge in these intense pressure and heat moments. Consider how your trials have led you closer to God, purifying your faith and making it more resilient. These trials, though difficult, serve as divine opportunities for growth and deepening your trust in God. They are not merely obstacles but are instrumental in perfecting your faith. By viewing trials through this lens, you can begin to welcome them as catalysts for spiritual and personal development, knowing that God uses them to mold you into a Reflection of His image.

Action Step

Identify a current trial and write down three lessons or strengths you've gained from it. Every day this week, thank God for one of these lessons, asking Him to continue refining your faith through this trial.

The Eternity in Each Moment

Scripture Reading

- Ephesians 5:15-16 (NIV): "Be very careful, then, how you live—not as unwise but as wise, making the most of every opportunity, because the days are evil."

Reflection

We Don't Know Who Needs to Hear this, but live your life with purpose and measure!

Ephesians stresses the importance of living wisely and maximizing every opportunity. Our modern lives are often packed with activities, deadlines, and digital distractions. It's easy to lose sight of what's truly important. Paul's advice—given so many centuries ago—reminds us to carefully consider how we invest our time, emphasizing that truly valuable opportunities are ones that align with God's purpose for us.

Prayer

Dear God, help me to discern how to use my time wisely. May I prioritize what truly matters and not get lost in the distractions of daily life. Give me the wisdom to seek and seize opportunities that bring me closer to You and help further Your kingdom.

In Jesus' name, we pray.

Amen.

Contemplation

Consider the time we often spend on social media, streaming shows, or engaging in activities that don't necessarily add value to our spiritual or personal growth. Even though not all leisure activities are bad, our intentions behind them matter. When was the last time you paused to truly embrace a moment, whether it was seeking God's presence in prayer, enjoying nature, or sharing a meaningful conversation with a loved one? Time is a limited resource. Reflecting on how you spend it can reveal areas where you might be spreading yourself thin or missing out on meaningful moments. God has placed eternity in our hearts (Ecclesiastes 3:11), encouraging us to seek lasting joy and purpose each minute. Make each moment count by aligning it with His will and purpose.

Action Step

This week, conduct a time audit. Keep track of how you spend each hour for at least one day. At the end of the day, reflect on your activities. Identify an hour that could be better spent. Consider dedicating that time to prayer, helping someone in need, or engaging in a spiritual discipline such as Bible study. Remember, each hour is an opportunity to grow closer to God and fulfill His purpose for you.

Netflix and Chill: Time to Rest

Scripture Reading

- Matthew 11:28-30 (NIV): "Come to me, all you who are weary and burdened, and I will give you rest. Take my yoke upon you and learn from me, for I am gentle and humble in heart, and you will find rest for your souls. For my yoke is easy and my burden is light."

Reflection

We Don't Know Who Needs to Hear this, but taking time for yourself is okay!

In our fast-paced world, rest seems like a luxury. We often feel we must be doing something productive every moment, which leads to burnout and stress. Jesus offers us an invitation to rest in Him, a rest that goes deeper than physical relaxation. It's about finding peace for our souls. His yoke is easy, meaning His expectations are not burdensome but life-giving. He calls us to lay down our burdens and embrace His way of living, prioritizing rest and spiritual renewal.

Prayer

Lord Jesus, teach me to rest in You amid my hectic life. Help me understand that true rest comes from surrendering my worries and burdens to You. Remind me that being constantly busy does not define my worth. Thank You for giving me rest for my soul.

In Jesus' name, we pray.

Amen.

Contemplation

Think about how often you push through exhaustion because of your to-do list. How many times have you sacrificed meaningful moments with God to get things done? God is not calling us to a never-ending hustle. He is calling us to balance, peace, and rest. The concept of Sabbath, a day of rest, is rooted in creation. God rested from His work, setting an example for us. Reflect on the quality of your rest. True rest doesn't just mean sleeping or relaxing physically, but also resting in God's presence, where we can unload our stresses and receive His comfort and peace. Imagine how your life might change if you made rest a spiritual discipline instead of something you only get to do when you collapse from exhaustion.

Action Step

Set aside one day this week as a true day of rest. No work, no errands, no to-do lists—just rest. Spend quality time with God, read a favorite scripture, walk in nature, or simply be still. Make this a regular practice to experience the depth of rest Jesus promises.

SEASONS OF WAITING

Scripture Reading

- ☐ Ecclesiastes 3:1 (NIV): "There is a time for everything, and a season for every activity under the heavens."

Reflection

We Don't Know Who Needs to Hear this, but your potential is limitless!

Life can seem like an endless series of transitions. We have moments of excitement, joy, sadness, and waiting. Ecclesiastes encourages us by affirming that each phase has its place and purpose. This wisdom speaks to the heart of our human experience, reminding us that waiting is not just a period of inactivity but a season for something meaningful. Whether we are waiting for a job, a relationship, or a sign from God, these periods can be filled with purpose if we trust in God's timing.

Prayer

Heavenly Father, help me to trust in Your perfect timing. In seasons of waiting, grant me patience and open my eyes to the lessons and growth You have planned for me. Teach me to embrace these periods as opportunities to deepen my faith and character.

In Jesus' name, we pray.

Amen.

Contemplation

We often see waiting as a negative experience, something to endure until the next thing comes. However, every season serves its purpose in God's greater plan. When you're in a season of waiting, it's crucial to recognize that God is working behind the scenes, preparing you for what's next. It's during these waiting periods that our character is tested and refined. Much like a farmer waits for the right time to harvest crops, we must understand that rushing can often spoil the blessing to come. Imagine the patience of God, who has seen everything from the beginning of time. He knows the exact moment when things should unfold in our lives.

Reflect on how you have navigated seasons of waiting in the past. Did you trust God during those times or try to rush His plans? This Reflection can help you better embrace and find peace during your current season of waiting.

Action Step

Instead of feeling frustrated, make a list of lessons and insights you are gaining during your current or next period of waiting. Write down one thing you are thankful for daily and how you see God working in your waiting season. This practice will help you shift your focus from impatience to gratitude and growth.

Using Time Wisely

Scripture Reading

- Psalm 90:12 (NIV) Teach us to number our days, that we may gain a heart of wisdom;

Reflection

We Don't Know Who Needs to Hear this, but remember to make each moment count!

The psalmist's prayer is a humble request for the wisdom to live with an awareness of time's fleeting nature. Numbering our days promotes intentional living, making us more conscious of how we spend our hours. In an age of endless distractions, wisdom calls us to use our time judiciously. Recognizing the impermanence of life can inspire us to focus on what truly matters—relationships, growth, and our walk with God.

Prayer

Gracious God, grant me wisdom to number my days and use my time intentionally. Help me prioritize my time in ways that bring me closer to You and positively impact those around me. Guide me to live a life that reflects Your love and purpose.

In Jesus' name, we pray.

Amen.

Contemplation

Contemplate the impermanence of life and the limited number of days we have. How often do we get caught up in trivial pursuits, neglecting what genuinely substances our soul and spirit? Numbering our days does not mean living in fear of death; rather, it means valuing each day as a precious gift from God. Our society often emphasizes productivity, but productive activity devoid of purpose can lead to an unfulfilled life. Analyze how you spend a typical day. Are your actions anchored in eternal significance or revolving around temporary gains? Living life to the fullest is not about cramming more activities into your day; instead, it's about making each activity count. Jesus lived only 33 years on Earth, but His every moment was filled with purpose. Reflect on how you can bring more substance and meaning to your daily routine.

Action Step

Create a mission statement for your life that reflects your core values and God's purpose for you. Use this statement to guide your daily activities. As you plan your week, ensure that your tasks and commitments align with this mission. Make an effort to include quality time for relationships, personal growth, and spiritual disciplines. Keep returning to your mission statement whenever you feel overwhelmed or directionless.

Discernment

Scripture Reading

- 1 Corinthians 2:15 (NASB2020): "But the one who is spiritual discerns all things, yet he himself is discerned by no one."

- James 1:5 (NASB2020): "But if any of you lacks wisdom, let him ask of God, who gives to all generously and without reproach, and it will be given to him."

Reflection

We Don't Know Who Needs to Hear this, but learn to listen to your inner voice!

In our fast-paced and often tumultuous world, the gift of discernment is a precious blessing. Discernment, as described in Scripture, is more than mere judgment or decision-making; it is the ability to perceive and understand God's will and guidance in every situation. It's the spiritual insight that allows us to navigate through life's complexities with wisdom and clarity.

Discernment involves more than just knowing what is right or wrong. It is an inner wisdom the Holy Spirit gives that helps us distinguish between the good, the better, and the best. Discernment is also the quiet, steady voice that guides us to make choices that align with God's will rather than our fleeting desires or the world's pressures.

In 1 Corinthians 2:15, Paul speaks of the spiritual person who discerns all things. This discernment comes from a deep relationship with God, built through prayer, reading Scripture, and seeking His presence. It requires a heart attuned to the Holy Spirit, a heart that listens and responds to divine guidance. This is why James encourages us to ask God for wisdom. It is a gift that He gives generously, but we must be willing to seek it earnestly.

Prayer

Heavenly Father, I thank You for the gift of discernment. Help me to cultivate a heart that is sensitive to Your voice and to recognize Your guidance in every decision I make. Grant me wisdom to see beyond the surface and to understand Your will for my life. Teach me to rely on Your Word and the Holy Spirit to lead me in truth. May I always seek Your counsel and trust in Your perfect plan.

In Jesus' name, we pray.

Amen.

Contemplation

As you go about your day, take a moment to pause and seek God's guidance in the decisions you face. Ask Him to grant you discernment and to help you align your choices with His will. Reflect on areas where you may need clearer understanding or wisdom. Trust that God will provide the insight you need, and remember that true discernment comes from a deep and abiding relationship with Him.

Action Step

Identify one area in your life where you need greater discernment. Spend time in prayer and meditation, asking God for wisdom and clarity. Consider journaling your thoughts and any insights you receive, and seek advice from trusted spiritual mentors if needed. As you move forward, be attentive to how God leads and trust His perfect guidance.

Outro

We Don't Know Who Needs to Hear This But..., may you carry these reflections and inspirations with you into the world. While life will continue "life-ing," full of challenges, remember that the potential for growth, resilience, and profound transformation lies within every struggle.

Each devotion was crafted with you in mind, a reminder that even on the toughest days, there is a spark of hope waiting to be ignited. Embrace the power of your story, share your light with others, and never underestimate the impact you can have on those around you.

May you walk forward with renewed strength, knowing you are seen, valued, and loved. Keep seeking inspiration, nurturing your spirit, and uplifting others. Your journey matters, and every step you take is a testament to the beauty of perseverance. Thank you for allowing these words to accompany you.

We Don't Know Who Needs to Hear This But, you are empowered to push forward with courage and hope!

About the Authors

Danielle Robinson Smith has dedicated her life to servant leadership, consistently seeking roles that serve a purpose beyond herself. Her journey began after high school when she joined the federal government as a summer intern at the Department of the Air Force, working in the Records Management and Privacy Act Office. This experience ignited her pride in public service and set the stage for her future endeavors.

Danielle earned a Bachelor of Science in Management with a focus on Marketing from Hampton University in 2004. After graduation, she moved to Washington, D.C., to work at Walter Reed Army Medical Center. She is a certified Professional Coach, mediator, MBTI Practitioner, Human Capital Strategist, strategic workforce planner, and Lean Six Sigma Black Belt.

Beyond her professional achievements, her more cherished titles include Woman of God, Wife, and Mother! Danielle is a devoted wife to Randy Smith and a proud mother of two wonderful boys, Bryce and Jax. Family and legacy are central to her life, providing purpose and immense joy.

 Glenn Coleman is a retired Chief Master Sergeant of the United States Air Force with an impressive 26 years of dedicated service. His remarkable career was defined by his ability to lead teams with a servant-leader philosophy, prioritizing the growth and success of others before his own. This commitment to service shaped a legacy of excellence and mentorship.

Following his military career, Glenn continued his path of service by becoming an ordained minister. In this role, he translates his leadership skills and compassionate nature into spiritual guidance, providing support and counsel to individuals and communities alike. Glenn is dedicated to fostering an environment of empathy and support where members are encouraged to pursue their own paths of service and personal growth. His work in these areas demonstrates his enduring commitment to making a positive impact on the lives of others.

In addition to his professional accomplishments, Glenn Coleman's academic background highlights his dedication to self-improvement and lifelong learning. He holds a Bachelor's Degree in Applied Business Management, where he graduated with honors, earning Magna Cum Laude distinctions. Furthermore, he possesses a Master's Degree in Business Management with a concentration in Human Resources, equipping him with the expertise to manage and develop talent effectively. These educational achievements further empower Glenn to lead with knowledge and integrity, reinforcing his ability to serve his community and professional spheres excellently.

www.ingramcontent.com/pod-product-compliance
Lightning Source LLC
Chambersburg PA
CBHW032005080426
42735CB00007B/512